Guildtown Primary School
School Road
Guildtown
Perthshire PH2 6BX
Tel. 0821 640382

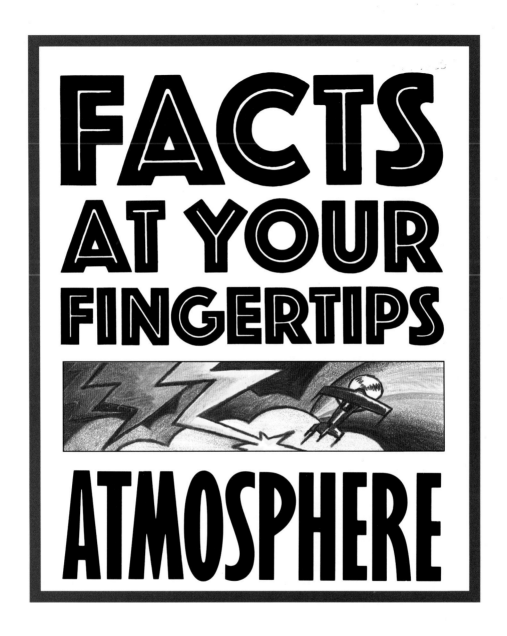

FACTS AT YOUR FINGERTIPS

ATMOSPHERE

DAVID MARSHALL

SIMON & SCHUSTER
YOUNG BOOKS

Commissioning editor: Daphne Butler
Design and artwork: SPL Design
Photographs: ZEFA, except for
FLPA (25t),
NHPA (15t, 16b, 17)
Spectrum (19t)
Typesetting and layout: Quark Xpress

First published in Great Britain in 1992
by Simon & Schuster Young Books

Simon & Schuster Young Books
Campus 400, Maylands Avenue
Hemel Hempstead, Herts HP2 7EZ

Printed and bound in Belgium
by Proost International Book Production

A catalogue record for this book
is available from the British Library
ISBN 0 7500 1086 X

CONTENTS

WHAT IS THE

ATMOSPHERE?

The atmosphere is an envelope of gases around the Earth which acts as a protective blanket keeping out the sun's most deadly rays. The mixture of gases is ideal for supporting life. No other planet in the solar system has the same atmosphere. ►

◄ The air above us has different layers. The troposphere is the one closest to the Earth and contains most of the gases. Here, all the weather occurs and the temperature drops 1°C with every 150 metres rise upwards.

Winds constantly circulate the air in the troposphere around the planet. Sometimes, huge storms called hurricanes or typhoons form. Today, satellites help us to track a storm and warn people living in the path that it is coming. ►

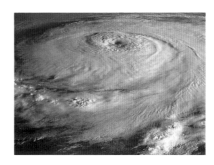

AIR PRESSURE

There are about 10,000 kilogrammes of air above each square metre of the Earth's surface. This weight presses down on the Earth with a force that we call air pressure. As you climb up a mountain, there is less air above you and so the air pressure falls. Air pressure changes from day to day and place to place. Wind blows from places of high pressure to places of low pressure to try to even it out.

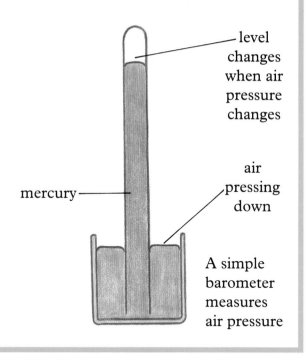

level changes when air pressure changes

air pressing down

mercury

A simple barometer measures air pressure

WATER VAPOUR

When water boils in a kettle it turns into water vapour. You can't see water vapour coming out of the spout, but as it cools in the air, it condenses forming a cloud that we call steam.

The amount of moisture in the atmosphere is known as the humidity. The warmer the air is, the more moisture it can hold. When damp air cools, it cannot to hold as much moisture as before. Clouds, dew, frost or fog all happen when damp air cools down.

CLOUDS

Clouds are found in the first 10 kilometres of the atmosphere. They form when warm, damp air rises and cools—some clouds become so heavy with water that rain or snow falls. Heavy cloud acts like a blanket, making cloudy nights warm but keeping cloudy days cold.

Three types of cloud: *above*, low-lying stratus; *left*, flat-bottomed, fluffy cumulus; *below*, high cirrus swept into wisps by the wind.

◄ Some cumulus clouds billow up several kilometres in the air turning to dense storm clouds.

WINDS

Wind blows because the sun warms the Earth more in some places than others. The warm air rises and more air rushes in to fill the space. Winds often blow in set patterns across the world, but they also change their direction frequently. Winds blowing across the sea pick up water vapour which later falls as rain on the land.

The strength of the wind is often measured on a scale invented by Sir Francis Beaufort in 1805.

THE BEAUFORT SCALE

scale	wind	effect on the land
0	calm	smoke rises vertically
1	light air	smoke drifts on wind
2	light breeze	wind felt on face, leaves rustle
3	gentle breeze	leaves and twigs move/flags flutter
4	moderate breeze	raises dust and paper, moves small branches
5	fresh breeze	small trees in leaf begin to sway
6	strong breeze	large branches sway, difficulty with umbrellas
7	moderate gale	whole trees sway, walking difficult
8	fresh gale	twigs break off
9	strong gale	chimney pots and slates blown off
10	whole gale	trees uprooted, much damage to buildings
11	storm	widespread damage
12	hurricane	tropical revolving storms

THUNDER AND LIGHTNING

Thunder and lightning are caused by air currents inside storm clouds. Ice crystals, raindrops and hailstones crash into each other, making a massive negative charge collect at the bottom of the cloud. The charge builds up until a huge spark flies either down to the Earth or across to another part of the cloud. The thunder clap is the noise caused by the spark.

RAINBOWS

Rainbows are formed when sunlight passes through falling raindrops. White sunlight is split into the different colours of the spectrum just as it is when it passes through a prism.

LIVING IN

THE AIR

There are thousands of creatures flying around in the air. There are many insects—bees, wasps and butterflies—usually flying quite close to the ground, and birds of all shapes and sizes—some flying hundreds of miles each year. ➤

◄ When sunlight falls on the leaves of plants and trees, they release oxygen into the air. It is thought that much of the oxygen in the atmosphere was built up in this way. If we destroy the forests, we could upset the balance.

The air makes a 900 kilometre deep envelope around the Earth. It resembles the oceans—drifting harmlessly, blowing gently on us in some places and whirling with great violence in others. Without it we cannot live. ➤

ANIMALS BREATHE

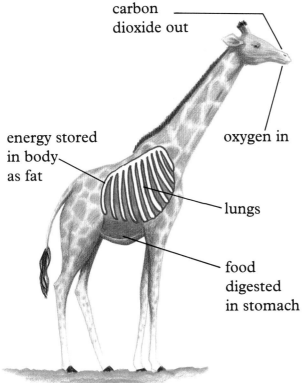

carbon dioxide out

oxygen in

energy stored in body as fat

lungs

food digested in stomach

Most animals breathe air in through their mouths and noses. The air passes down their windpipes and into their lungs. Here, it passes through smaller and smaller tubes to air sacs where oxygen can be absorbed into the blood stream.

The oxygen is needed to make energy from food stored in the body as fat. Carbon dioxide is made at the same time, and this is passed back to the lungs to be breathed out.

▲ Animals use oxygen to make energy from the food stored in their bodies as fats.

Animals that live in the sea must adapt the way they breathe. Sea mammals come up to the surface to breathe but can stay under water for a long time on one breath. Fish filter oxygen out of the water itself, through their gills.

Whales have holes in the tops of their heads through which they blow spent air when they are at the surface of the sea. ►

PLANTS RESPIRE

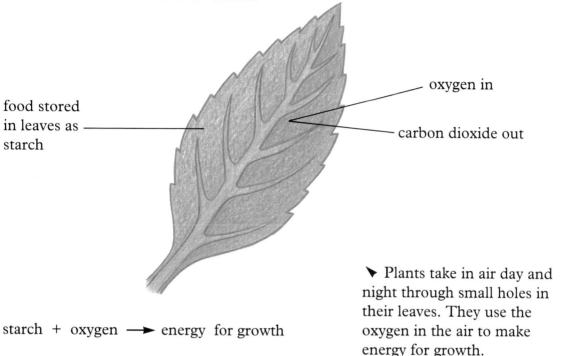

food stored
in leaves as
starch

oxygen in

carbon dioxide out

starch + oxygen ⟶ energy for growth

▼ Plants take in air day and
night through small holes in
their leaves. They use the
oxygen in the air to make
energy for growth.

Plants breathe by taking
air in through small holes
in their leaves. They use
the oxygen from the air with
the food stored in their leaves
to make energy for growth.
Like animals, they breathe out
carbon dioxide. In plants, this
process is called respiration.

Plants don't all grow at the
same rate. Like animals,
some plants grow faster
than others. ►

PHOTOSYNTHESIS

light from the sun falls on the leaves

leaves contain green substance called chlorophyll

leaves take in carbon dioxide from the air

leaves make food for the plant from carbon dioxide and water with the help of chlorophyll and sunlight

leaves give out oxygen

roots take in water which travels up the stems to the leaves

Animals must gather their food, but plants make their own by a process called photosynthesis. They take carbon dioxide from the air and water from the ground, turning it into starch which they store in their leaves. To make this happen, plants use the energy in sunlight and the green substance in their leaves which is called chlorophyll. Photosynthesis does not take place at night because there is no sunlight.

SPREADING SEED

Plants need a way of spreading their seed, otherwise many plants will be trying to grow on the same patch of ground. Dandelion and thistle seeds, have fluffy, hairy tufts that act like parachutes to carry the seeds away on the wind.
Old man's beard has fruit with long hairy tails that catch the wind. Trees such as ash, birch and maple, have winged seeds that act like helicopter blades. The seeds spin to the ground some distance away from the parent tree.

▲ Maple seeds hang in clusters ripening in the sun. When ready they will float away on the wind.

◄ Dandelions flower many times between spring and autumn. Each single flower has hundreds of seeds which are borne away on the wind to find fresh ground.

BIRDS

A bird can fly through the air by gliding or by flapping its wings. When flapping its wings, it changes the angle of some of the feathers. On the upstroke, the feathers turn to allow the air to pass through, and on the downstroke the feathers close to push against the air and propel the bird upward and forward. When gliding the wing feathers are closed to gain lift from the air currents.

▲ Young birds learn to fly by instinct once their wing feathers have grown.

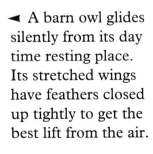

◄ A barn owl glides silently from its day time resting place. Its stretched wings have feathers closed up tightly to get the best lift from the air.

FLYING INSECTS

Most flying insects have two pairs of wings which they beat up and down when they fly. Each wing can move on its own, independently from the others, so the insect can steer itself in a chosen direction.

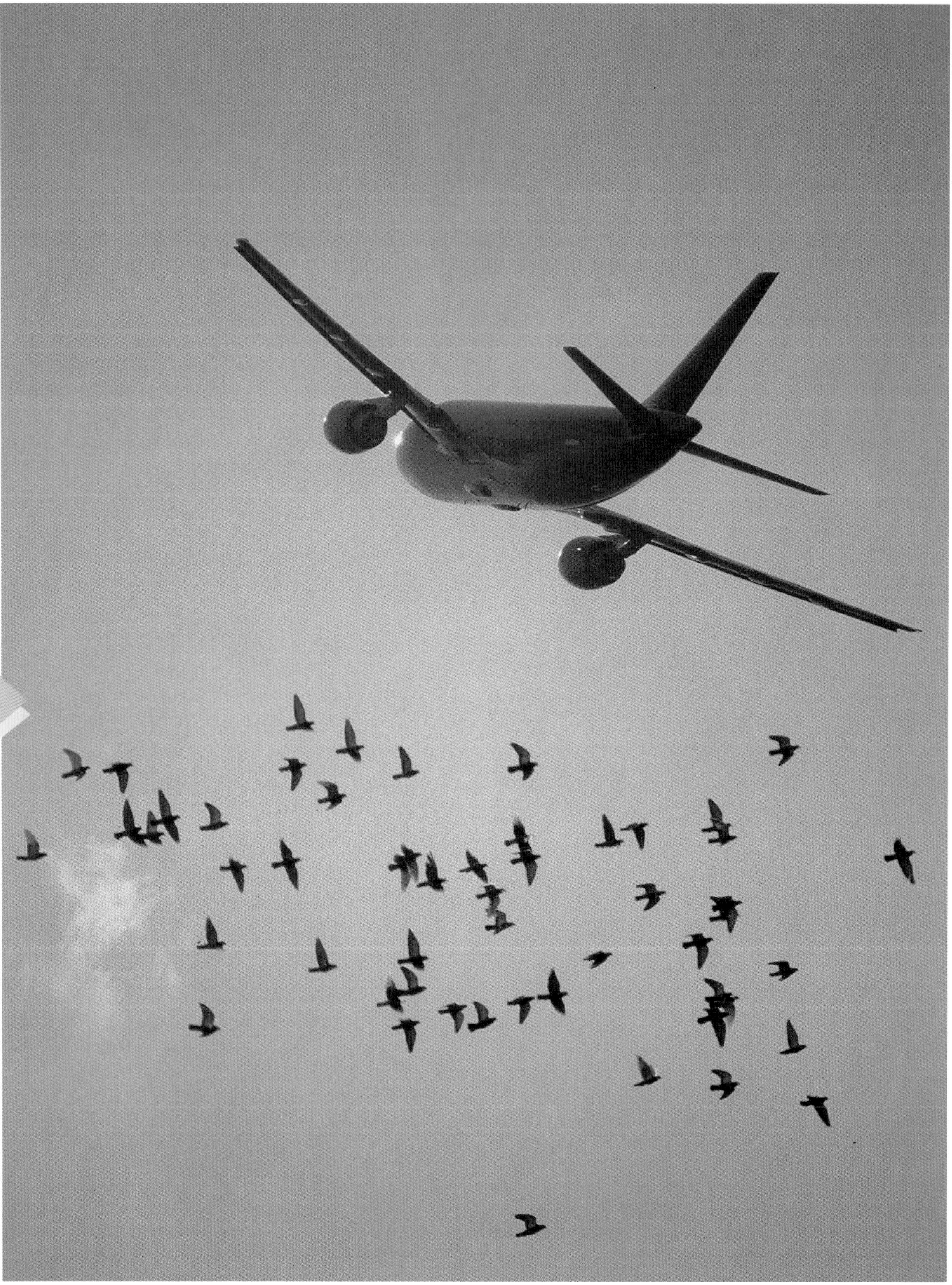

HOW WE USE

THE AIR

If there was no air, we would live in a silent world. Sound needs air to travel through. Many musical instruments work by forcing streams of air through narrow tubes. Inside the tubes the air vibrates creating sound. ➤

◄ The wind contains great power. For centuries we have harnessed this power to do work for us. Modern windmills help boost electricity supplies without the harmful pollution caused by burning coal and oil.

We have started to learn only recently how we are destroying the quality of our air. We have used it as a catch-all sink for factory waste that will probably pollute the atmosphere for generations to come. ➤

FLOATING

Hot-air balloons were the first means of air travel. They can only go where the wind takes them and they are usually unable to return to their launch site. Balloons are open at the bottom but have a burner in the gap. The burner makes the air inside expand, some of the air spills out, the balloon becomes lighter than the surrounding air, and it floats upwards.

20

▲ Ballooning is popular, but expensive. Because balloons have no engines, they float silently above the ground.

◄ At the launch site, the balloon starts off flat. It must be carefully inflated with the air which is heated to make it expand and turn the balloon upright.

GLIDING

◄ Parascenders launch themselves into the air from the tops of cliffs. They can change direction, but need currents of air to go up and down.

A glider has no engine and must be pulled into the air by a light plane. It can be steered like a normal aircraft but like a parascender relies on currents of air to go up and down. ▼

Gliders and parascenders make use of upward rising currents of air called thermals. They circle round in the current gaining height as they go. Then glide gently back down to Earth. In 1961, a glider reached the record height of 14,102 metres. Birds also make use of thermals. In 1988, a greater snow goose hit a jumbo jet flying at nearly 11,000 metres.

AIRPLANES

An airplane needs three things for flight. An engine to drive it forward fast enough to take off and stay in the air. Wings to give it lift—with flaps to bank it left and right and to control the speed. And a tail to act as a rudder to turn it left and right, and with flaps which when lowered make it rise and when lifted make it descend.

▲ A Boeing 747 landing with the flaps down—this helps it fly at low speeds.

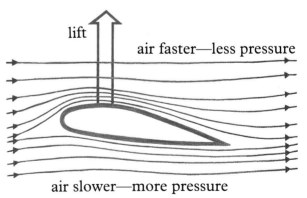

▲ Airplane wings are shaped so there is more pressure on the bottom of the wings and this pressure keeps the plane in the air.

HELICOPTERS

The blades on a helicopter's main rotor are like the wings on an airplane. They rotate at high speed and when tilted downward, they lift the helicopter up in the air. By changing the angle of the blades, the helicopter goes up or down, left or right, forward, or can hover above one spot.

With just one rotor, the body of the helicopter would try to twist in the opposite direction. So helicopters have a second small rotor at the back which makes them stable. Some larger helicopters have two large rotors, which rotate in opposite directions.

▲ Because helicopters can turn in small spaces and hover above one spot, they can reach places that might otherwise be impossible.

COMMUNICATION

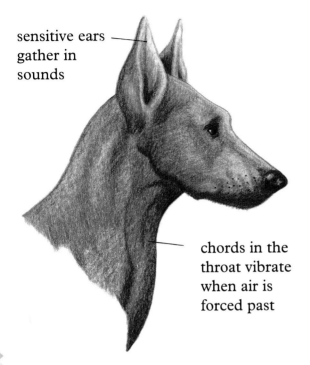

sensitive ears gather in sounds

chords in the throat vibrate when air is forced past

We communicate by talking to each other. That is by making a series of sounds. Sounds are made by anything that vibrates. If a wasp is buzzing near you, you hear the vibration of its wings. When a violin is playing, it is the vibration of the strings that you hear.

Sound travels through the air as waves which are caused by these vibrations. Out in space there is no sound because there is no air to vibrate. You hear sound because small bones inside your ear pick up the vibrations and send messages to your brain.

▲ Dogs like many other creatures make a noise by forcing air past chords in their throats. They hear noises by collecting sounds with their sensitive ears.

loudspeaker makes sound

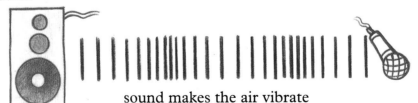

microphone picks up the vibrations in the air

sound makes the air vibrate

▲ We can turn sound waves into electrical waves which can be stored (on disc or tape) or transmitted long distances. We can then turn them back into the same sound whenever we want to hear their message.

WINDMILLS

Windmills are a way of capturing the power of the wind and using it for work, such as grinding corn. Windmills were invented round about AD 640. At first, the blades were like the sails of a boat, and drove flat, horizontal wheels. Later, the blades were put upright like a propellor. A windmill works best when the blades are facing into the wind. A smaller set of blades at the back of the mill makes sure the mill turns round so that the main blades always catch the full strength of the wind.

▲ In the days before the invention of engines powered by steam or electricity, wind was one of the few sources of power available to people.

Modern windmills are used to generate electricity and can have blades that are 60 metres long. They are mounted on towers about 100 metres high. Often a whole forests of windmills are put on one very windy site.

◄ Today, windmills are coming back into fashion. The have become a clean silent way of making electricity. They cannot make enough to replace the power stations—but every little helps.

TOXIC FUMES

◄ Gases released into the air as industrial waste are carried away by the wind. But they pollute the air causing acid rain and turning fog into smog.

Trees help to keep the balance between oxygen and carbon dioxide in the air. Acid rain falling on forests damages the trees. The leaves or needles turn brown and the trees slowly die. ▼

Fumes from car exhausts and factories contain many gases that have a harmful effect on the air, and the animals and plants that breathe it. Carbon monoxide, nitrous oxide and sulphur dioxide poison the air. Especially dangerous are the 450,000 tonnes of lead that are released in the exhaust gases of cars using leaded petrol.

RADIOACTIVE FALL OUT

Radioactivty can upset the chemistry of your body and make you very ill. People who handle radioactive materials wear heavy duty protective clothing. ►

▲ There are no waste gases when using nuclear energy as fuel in power stations but leaks of radioactivity are exceedingly dangerous.

A nuclear accident could mean that farm animals remain contaminated for many years. ▼

Nuclear power stations are built to make sure that leaks of radioactivity never happen. But still, in 1986, there was a dreadful accident at a power station at Chernobyl in Russia. More than 30 people died, 250 had severe radiation burns and 135,000 people had to leave their homes. Dust from the explosion was carried thousands of miles to other countries by the wind.

GREENHOUSE EFFECT

When sunshine falls on a greenhouse some of the heat gets caught inside and bounces around unable to get out. The temperature rises rapidly and unless you open the door to let fresh air in, the plants inside will wilt and die.

Plants grow well in the warm atmosphere of a greenhouse as long as there is plenty of moisture, and they are shaded from the full force of the sun. ➤

Carbon dioxide is one of the gases in the air. If frozen carbon dioxide is put in a beaker, it quickly evaporates and disappears ▼

The Earth acts very like a gigantic greenhouse. When we burn oil and coal, carbon dioxide forms. This collects as a layer high in the atmosphere.
The heat from the sun warms the Earth during the day and much is reflected back to space during the night. A layer of carbon dioxide keeps some of the warmth in, so the atmosphere heats up just a tiny bit each day. It is possible that over the next 150 years the temperature could rise by 4°C.

OZONE LAYER

Between 20 and 40 kilometres above the Earth, the air is rich in a gas called ozone. The ozone is there because the sun's radiation excites oxygen atoms, making them join up in threes instead of twos. The ozone protects Earth from much of the dangerous radiation from the sun. Without the ozone, life as we know it could not exist.

Some years ago, scientists discovered a group of chemicals that worked very well in refrigerators and aerosol spray cans. We have stopped using them now, because we have discovered that they destroy ozone, and could be making holes in the ozone layer.

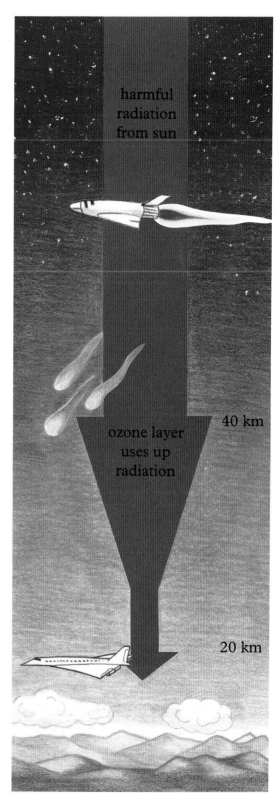

harmful radiation from sun

ozone layer uses up radiation

40 km

20 km

FACTS ABOUT THE AIR

The sky is not really blue. It is black. However, the sun's rays travelling down through the atmosphere hit molecules of gas and are scattered by them giving a bright bluish colour.

We each breathe the air millions of times in a year. Air contains tiny particles of salt, chemicals, minerals, ash and minute fragments from meteors.

Germs and bacteria in air are far too small for us to see. About 656 million of the smallest bacteria can fit onto the head of a pin. In a city at rush hour over 375 million particles can be taken in every lungful of air.

When you sneeze up to a million tiny droplets fly out of your mouth and nose into the air. They mix with all the other tiny particles. Ten thousands particles blow around in every cubic centimetre of air.

The air carries enough pollen from plants to cover every square metre of the Earth's surface every year with 100 million grains.

On the Earth's surface, air pressure is the equivalent of 10 tonnes on every human being.

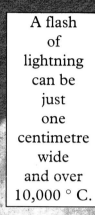

When tiny droplets of water freeze in a cloud they may join together to make a snowflake. Snow flakes are always six sided and each one has a different shape.

A flash of lightning can be just one centimetre wide and over 10,000 ° C.

A rainbow's position can never be fixed. Everyone sees their own personal rainbow from wherever they are standing. A rainbow is always seen as part of a circle. Sometimes from an airplane you can see the whole circle.

Air is a mixture of gases—about 78% nitrogen, 21% oxygen, 0.9% argon and 0.1% others. Carbon dioxide is now about 0.035% of the atmosphere—and increasing.

On the top of mount Everest the pressure of air is less than a third of that at sea level.

There are 500 million, million (500,000,000,000,000) tonnes of water in our atmosphere at any one time. It sounds a lot but it is only 1000th of 1 per cent of all the water on Earth.

INDEX